CW00383994

FLINT
EWLOE

Derek Renn CBE, PhD, FSA[†]
and
Richard Avent MA, FSA[*]

Contents

Edited by David M. Robinson BSc, PhD, FSA
Designed by Joanna Griffiths

First Published 1995, Revised edition 2001

© Cadw: Welsh Historic Monuments (Crown Copyright),
Crown Building, Cathays Park, Cardiff CF10 3NQ.

Printed in Great Britain by South Western Printers

ISBN 1 85760 182 3

A HISTORY OF THE CASTLES

INTRODUCTION

The castles of Flint and Ewloe lie just five miles (8km) apart, and they were probably constructed within twenty years of one another. Although they have one feature in common - a great tower or *donjon* - the fortifications at each site are very different in layout and detail. These differences reflect the origins and purpose of the two castles. Ewloe was a native Welsh stronghold, built by a prince of Gwynedd at a time when the surrounding area was absorbed into the orbit of power of his principality. By contrast, Flint was a fortress built to assure the domination of an area brought under firm English control; it might also be used as a springboard for further invasion in north Wales. The story of the two castles is also a reflection of the fate of Llywelyn ap Gruffudd, the first and last native prince of all Wales, who strove to create a principality largely independent of the English Crown.

In the late 1250s, Llywelyn had made common cause with the English barons opposing King Henry III's government style. He had recovered the Welsh district or *cantref* of Tegeingl (the area of much of modern Flintshire) by force from the Crown's officers in 1257, and he began to build a new castle at Ewloe. Under the Treaty of Montgomery (1267), the king acknowledged Llywelyn's title as Prince of Wales. The king was his overlord, but Llywelyn effectively ruled much of the land of Wales. On the death of Henry III in 1272, however, the new king, Edward I, proved to be much more formidable than his father had been. In July 1277, King Edward began 'combined operations' against Prince Llywelyn, setting up a fortified beachhead at Flint for the invasion of Gwynedd. Within a few months, Llywelyn's power was restricted to the heart of Snowdonia and the island of Anglesey. His period of triumph had turned to one of disaster in the space of a decade. Five years later, a widespread uprising against English domination was sparked off by Llywelyn's brother, Dafydd. A second royal invasion was to lead to the tragic deaths of both princes, and to the final collapse of organized Welsh resistance to the English Crown.

Left: *A general view of Ewloe Castle, built 'in the corner of the wood' by Llywelyn ap Gruffudd about 1257. The so-called Welsh Tower, which probably functioned as a keep, is the most prominent feature of the site.*

3

BORDER CONFLICT

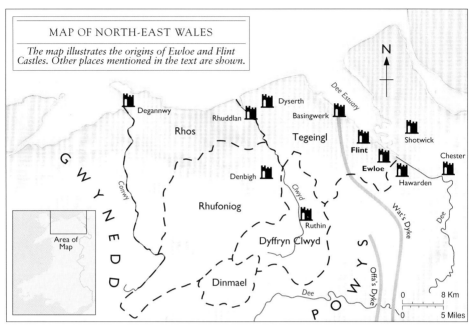

MAP OF NORTH-EAST WALES

The map illustrates the origins of Ewloe and Flint Castles. Other places mentioned in the text are shown.

The region between the rivers Clwyd and Dee, the extreme north-east corner of Wales, still bears much physical evidence of its history as a border zone. It comprised the old Welsh *cantref*, or district, of Tegeingl, and formed part of a 'debatable land' - 'The Middle Country' (*Y Berfeddwlad*) - between two nations. The four *cantrefs* which composed 'The Middle Country' (Dyffryn Clwyd, Rhos, Rhufoniog and Tegeingl) were surrounded to the south and west by the major principalities of Gwynedd and Powys (see map), this vulnerable area as a whole was frequently fought over by the native Welsh princes themselves. It was also a natural target for English advance westward from Chester. Indeed, long before

the arrival of the Normans on this part of the bord the pendulum of Saxon or Welsh supremacy had swung to and fro for centuries.

THE NORMAN ADVANCE

Following the battle of Hastings in 1066, William the Conqueror's policy for the Welsh border wa to establish a series of marcher lordships, with the principal centres at Chester, Shrewsbury and Hereford. King William had the castle of Chester built in 1070 and granted the earldom, which was t

The coastal strip of north Wales was always vulnerable to Norman and English attack. In the early 1070s, Hugh of Avranches, earl of Chester, and Robert his deputy consolidated their hold on the north-eastern borderlands with the construction of a 'mott and bailey' stronghold at Rhuddlan. This detail of Norman knights comes from the Bayeux Tapestry.

*n the
tings of
ald of
'es (d. 1223),
eems the
n of north
les were
ecially skilful
h long spears.
's illustration of a
teenth-century
lsh spearman comes
m the Littere Wallie
opyright: Public Record
fice, E 36/274).*

lude the Dee valley, to Hugh of Avranches, known
Hugh the Fat (d. 1101). Earl Hugh's deputy,
obert, had soon established a base with an earth
d timber castle at Rhuddlan, and his forces
netrated along the coastal strip of north Wales
vards Anglesey, building castles as they went. But
1094, the Welsh united against the common
emy and inflicted a series of major defeats on the
ormans. It was Gruffudd ap Cynan (d. 1137),
cording to his later biographer, who 'delivered the
d of Gwynedd from castles'.

In fact, although the Norman conquest of
gland took just five years, the Anglo-Norman
vances into Wales were to continue for the next
o centuries. Mountainous Snowdonia, at the heart
the principality of Gwynedd, was to prove the
mest base of Welsh resistance. In 1114, three
mies under King Henry I (1100-35) converged on
e region and temporarily halted the expansion of
ruffudd ap Cynan. But by 1157 Gruffudd's son,
wain (d. 1170), had established himself on
e southern shore of the Dee when he
ibushed King Henry II (1154-89) at a
adblock near Coleshill. Henry escaped
d pushed forward until Owain sued for
ace. During the next ten years, however,
wain was to recapture the castles of
iuddlan and Basingwerk, and an English
vading army was defeated by appalling
eather conditions in the Berwyn
ountains in 1165.

Under Gruffudd ap Cynan and his son,
wain, Gwynedd had enjoyed a golden
a with the strength of the family dynasty
uilt up gradually but effectively. On
wain's death in 1170 the fragility of this
ccess was exposed. According to Welsh
stom, his lands were divided among his
rviving sons; there followed thirty years
oft-times bloody family strife.

LLYWELYN AB IORWERTH

Llywelyn ab Iorwerth - Llywelyn 'the Great'
(d. 1240) - was the grandson of Owain Gwynedd.
His rise to power was meteoric: like 'the swirl of a
great windstorm', as one of his court poets put it.
Llywelyn swept aside uncles and cousins and secured
recognition of his position from King John (1199-
1216) in 1201. Indeed, in 1205, he married John's
illegitimate daughter, Joan. But relations between
Llywelyn and his father-in-law were strained more
than once, and in 1211 the king - outraged by
Llywelyn's insubordination - led two invasion forces
into north Wales, penetrating with devastating effect
deep into Gwynedd. The following year, John
assembled a huge army and seemed intent on
complete conquest. At the last moment, the king
abandoned the campaign, with rumours of a threat
against his life playing no small part in the decision.

After John's death, Llywelyn continued to extend
his power and influence throughout Wales. He
proved a master at exploiting the divisions between
and within the English
marcher families of the
borders, and used his
children to secure several
important alliances. In the
north, for example, the
marriage of his daughter,
Helen, to John 'the Scot'
(d. 1237) formed such an
alliance with the earls of
Chester.

*Above: King John (1199-1216)
led two invasion forces into
north Wales against Llywelyn
ab Iorwerth which penetrated
with devastating effect, deep
into the heartlands of
Gwynedd. This manuscript
illustration of the king by
Matthew Paris dates from the
1250s (By kind permission of
the British Library, Royal Ms.
14 C VII, f. 9).*

*Left: For the first forty years of
the thirteenth century Llywelyn
ab Iorwerth (d. 1240)
dominated the whole of Wales.
Apart from temporary
setbacks, he had effective
control over the entire north-
eastern borderlands. This stone
head found at Deganwy
Castle is thought to represent
the prince (By permission of the
National Museum of Wales).*

Left: *During the long reign of King Henry III (1216-72), much royal energy was devoted to curbing the expansionist policies of Llywelyn ab Iorwerth and Llywelyn ap Gruffudd. This illustration of the king is from his gilt-bronze tomb-effigy in Westminster Abbey (By courtesy of the Dean and Chapter of Westminster).*

On John's death, however, King Henry III (1216-72) acquired the earldom of Chester, which included the castles of Chester itself, and that of Shotwick which lay just across the Dee from the later Flint. Indeed, this was to prove a significant tactical advantage since the Crown now had a direct foothold on the borders of Wales. Chester provided the direct base from which the Crown might confront the power of Gwynedd and curb its ambitions in the border zone.

Within a year of Llywelyn ab Iorwerth's death in 1240 his son, Dafydd, had been driven out of Tegeingl by Henry III who built a new stone castle at Dyserth. Dafydd died in 1246 and again within a

year his heirs - his nephews Owain and Llywelyn ap Gruffudd - had no option but to agree to the Treaty of Woodstock. All of north Wales to the east of the river Conwy was now in royal hands. Henry III granted the earldom of Chester and its castles to his eldest son, Edward (later King Edward I), in 1254. In doing so, he was also handing over what were to become further Welsh problems for the Crown; problems which were to take another thirty years to resolve.

LLYWELYN AP GRUFFUDD AND THE BUILDING OF EWLOE

Llywelyn ap Gruffudd (d. 1282) - Llywelyn the Last - was the grandson of Llywelyn ab Iorwerth. In 1255, he defeated his brothers, Owain (d. 1282) and Dafydd (d. 1283), in battle and set about reasserting the authority of Gwynedd. He recovered his family's manor of Ewloe as part of the *cantref* of Tegeingl in 1257, and he 'built a castle in

EWLOE CASTLE: DATING AND CONSTRUCTION

The only contemporary reference to a castle at Ewloe is to be found in a documentary source known as the *Chester Plea Rolls*, where, in a report made to King Edward II in 1311, Payn Tibotot, justice of Chester, summarizes the history of the manor of Ewloe from the middle of the twelfth century. He records that by 1257 Llywelyn ap Gruffudd had regained Ewloe from the English and 'built a castle in the corner of the wood'. In 1311 this was 'in great part standing'.

The site of the present castle bears some resemblance to that of a 'motte and bailey', with the so-called Welsh Tower situated on top of the raised area of the 'motte'. This has led to a suggestion that the first castle on the site may have been erected in the middle of the twelfth century by Owain Gwynedd (d. 1170). But there is a distinct lack of evidence to support this theory, and it seems most unlikely that such a site - where the topography has such a strong

natural slope - would have been suitable for the construction of an earthwork castle.

There have also been differences of opinion over the phasing of the construction of the stone castle. The first detailed interpretation of the castle was published in 1928, and was based on evidence that had been revealed during its clearance and consolidation. At that time, Ewloe was considered to have been built entirely by Llywelyn ap Gruffudd, from about 1257 onwards. Twenty years later, a new interpretation was presented. The Welsh Tower was now seen as the work of Llywelyn ab Iorwerth, dating to around 1210. Although apsidal in shape, the tower was thought to be similar to late

Left: *A report of 1311 in the Chester Plea Rolls records that Llywelyn ap Gruffudd regained Ewloe from the English in 1257 and proceeded to build a castle 'in the corner of the wood' (Copyright: Public Record Office, Plea Rolls, Chester 29/23, m. 48).*

corner of the wood' (see panel below); he later (1265) captured and
troyed the English castle in the area at Hawarden.

Llywelyn's success continued in 1258, with 'the magnates of Wales'
earing an oath of allegiance to him. It was now that he first assumed,
was accorded, the title 'Prince of Wales'. In the 1260s he supported
English baronial opposition to Henry III, and in 1267 the king -
hausted by repeated domestic difficulties - concluded a peace with
welyn. Under the Treaty of Montgomery sealed in that year, Llywelyn
ined the formal recognition of the title Prince of Wales for himself and
heirs. Territorially, he had gained control over much of the country,
h only the marcher lordships of the southern coastal region remaining
nly in English possession. In the north-east, although Hawarden Castle
s returned to English hands, it was not to be rebuilt for thirty years.

Left: *This aerial view of Ewloe shows the castle situated in its still dense woodland. In the medieval period it was part of the great forest of Ewloe.*

Right: *Llywelyn ap Gruffudd (d. 1282), the builder of Ewloe Castle. This sixteenth-century manuscript illustration shows the prince at an imaginary parliament (By gracious permission of Her Majesty the Queen, Royal Library, Wriothesley Ms. quire B).*

In the absence of any other solid evidence, we should perhaps accept the contemporary documentary account, and see the castle as a construction of Llywelyn ap Gruffudd in the years following 1257. The first stage of the works would have involved establishing a defensible position on the naturally strongest part of the site, the upper ward. To begin with, the area of the lower ward may have been used as a building compound surrounded by a timber palisade. In due course the timber defences would have been replaced by a stone curtain with a round tower included on the west side.

twelfth-century keeps on the English side of the border.

One feature of the building is perfectly clear: the curtain wall on the north and south sides of the lower ward abuts that surrounding the upper ward. This suggests that both the lower ward, and presumably the west tower, were added as a second phase in the building works. The earlier interpretation which placed the Welsh Tower as the primary structure on the site considered the upper and lower curtains to be contemporary, and belonging to the second phase. But unless three building phases were involved - first the Welsh Tower, then the upper curtain, and finally the lower ward - the balance of evidence points to all parts of the castle having been built during the same general period. None the less, the building could have been completed in two consecutive phases.

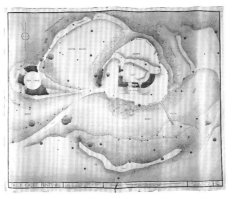

Left: *A ground plan of Ewloe Castle, prepared in 1921. Clearance on the site began the following year, with more of the original walls uncovered and consolidated. There have been differences of opinion over the phasing of the construction of the castle since the initial consolidation work was undertaken.*

Llywelyn's achievements to 1267 were quite remarkable, and no Welsh prince had commanded such power and influence since the coming of the Normans. But he was to remain at the pinnacle of his success for just ten years. Tensions quickly became evident in the March, and Llywelyn gradually found himself sidelined with a feeling that he was being defrauded of the gains he had won under the Treaty of Montgomery.

Exhausted by repeated domestic difficulties in England, King Henry III was forced to conclude a peace settlement with Llywelyn ap Gruffudd. Under the Treaty of Montgomery (1267), the king acknowledged Llywelyn's title as Prince of Wales (Copyright: Public Record Office, E 36/274, f. 327).

disturber of the peace'. Preparations for war took time, but by the following May a new great tower was under construction up on the old royal castle at Builth in mid Wales, and in July a new stronghold was begun at Aberystwyth. The whole campaign was carefully planned and executed, with up to 15,600 troops engaged in the royal force at its peak. Within a year of the declaration of war, Llywelyn had been comprehensively defeated and had been forced to accept the Treaty of Aberconwy. The bounds of his principality were pushed back into the heartlands of Gwynedd, with English control once more extending across north Wales as far as the river Conwy.

Right: *In his first war against Llywelyn ap Gruffudd, King Edward demonstrated that he had the will and the means to raise a military force on a scale unprecedented in medieval Britain. This near-contemporary manuscript illustration shows mounted knights engaged in battle (By kind permission of the British Library, Royal Ms. 16 G VI).*

Below: *A silver penny of King Edward I (1272-1307). In November 1276, following fruitless negotiations, the king declared his intention to go to war against Llywelyn ap Gruffudd 'as a rebel and disturber of the peace' (By courtesy of the Yorkshire Museum, York).*

KING EDWARD I AND THE OUTBREAK OF WAR

King Henry III died in 1272, whilst his heir was on crusade. At first, the accession of King Edward I (1272-1307) did not herald an immediate change in the fragile accord between the Crown and Prince Llywelyn, yet a conflict soon became inevitable. Llywelyn failed to swear fealty to the new king in 1273, and did not attend the king's formal coronation in the following year. Moreover, between December 1274 and April 1276, he failed to answer five summonses to do homage to Edward as his lord. The king was particularly enraged when, having journeyed to Chester in August 1275, he found that Llywelyn failed to turn up to perform homage.

In November 1276, after fruitless negotiations, Edward's patience gave out and he declared his intention to go against Llywelyn 'as a rebel and

THE BUILDING OF FLINT

...mid thirteenth-century manuscript illustration by Matthew Paris showing a king directing his master mason; construction work ...nderway in the background. Three years after the initial building work began at Flint, the king's brilliant mason-architect, ...es of St George, appeared on the building pay-roll in November 1280. He remained there for at least seventeen months ... kind permission of the British Library, Cotton Nero Ms. D I, f. 23v).

...t the start of the campaign, in June 1277, four ...of the king's clerks were despatched to recruit ...lding workers throughout the shires of midland ...gland. Supplies of tools and other equipment ...gan to be stockpiled at Chester. By the middle of ...y, Edward I himself was at Chester, where he was ...ned by the fleet from the Cinque Ports of the ...glish Channel. We are fortunate in that many of ...royal bills and accounts for this period survive, ...d we can put together a very clear picture of the ...y the king's programme of building works was ...nned and carried out.

...About 21 July, an army of soldiers, and another ...woodcutters and building workers from midland ...gland, who together had converged on Chester, ...oved forward to Flint. By this time, we must ...sume that Llywelyn's castle at Ewloe had fallen to ...e English, and was never again to be used as a ...tified stronghold.

Meanwhile, timber had been cut in the king's Cheshire woods, and in his brother's forest of Toxteth. It was brought to Flint - much of it on newly-made rafts - and a wooden palisade was raised. The site of Flint was selected for the first field headquarters because it was about a day's march along the ancient Roman road from Chester and because of its accessibility to sea-going ships. Beyond Flint, another day's journey away, lay Rhuddlan. There, the old Norman castle still survived as a major earthwork, and it was now to become the site of a great stone fortification. More specifically, the siting of Flint was determined by the location of a promontory of rock situated in an otherwise marshy estuary. Like all the other new towns and castles built for King Edward I in Wales during subsequent years, the accessibility of Flint by sea as well as land, reduced the chances of a successful siege in time of war.

An aerial view of Flint looking south-west in 1956. Along with the powerful castles, adjacent 'plantation boroughs' formed a very significant aspect of King Edward I's strategy for conquest and settlement in north Wales. At Flint, the borough was plann alongside the castle from the very outset (see panel, p. 20). On this virgin site, it was possible to lay out the town de novo, givi the planners the opportunity to produce a symmetrical grid pattern to the streets - a pattern which remains fossilized in the tou today (Crown Copyright, Photograph by courtesy of the Cambridge University Collection, TJ18).

The name *Le Flynt* for this virgin site may simply refer to its rocky nature in an otherwise marshy area, but we should not overlook the fact that Edward I incorporated symbolism into many of his castles. At Rhuddlan, for example, the river Clwyd was straightened by an expensive feat of engineering so that the new castle might adjoin the earlier English fortified site, and yet be accessible to seagoing ships. Conwy Castle and its walled borough were set up on the site of the Cistercian abbey where Llywelyn ab Iorwerth had been buried. The new works there also incorporated a building known as Llywelyn's Hall, which may have been the place where the armistice terms were drawn up after the 1276-77 war. And at Caernarfon, the king's castle not only enclosed the original Norman motte, but was intended as the 'new Constantinople', decorated with bands of coloured masonry, golden gates, and eagles on its towers like those of the eastern capital of the Roman empire. In this context, it has been suggested that t name *Le Flynt* may have been an allusion to Edward's intention to strike a spark of fire whose flames would consume Llywelyn.

The first construction workforce at *Le Flynt* included 970 diggers, plus many more latecomers, including 300 from the Lincolnshire fens who had been escorted by three mounted soldiers to preven their desertion *en route*. By the end of August 127 the digging force had reached 2,300. At first, there were also 300 woodcutters and 330 carpenters. Within a month, having completed the necessary temporary buildings, most of them moved on to th next camp at Rhuddlan. They cut back the woods beside the route as they went, thereby reducing potential cover for any Welsh attack on further supply trains.

The enormous force of navvies assembled at Fli was needed to dig a defensive ditch around the site

ected for the new castle and town, which was to
ome a fortified *bastide* (see panel below). The
gers worked with all speed, collecting
rformance pay' with bonuses for good work and
ductions for absenteeism. With the bulk of the
rk completed, most of the diggers moved on.
rgage plots in the town for new settlers were being

granted by February 1278, and by 1292, there were
seventy-four such settlers or burgesses in Flint
wealthy enough to be taxed. Among those landlords
holding burgage plots was the king's tailor (who had
been responsible for much of the provisioning for the
royal forces), along with several of the building
masters who had been engaged on building the castle.

BASTIDES OR PLANTED TOWNS

A *bastide* (French: *bâtir* - to build)
was the medieval word for a new
town planted in open country. They
were often laid out with straight
streets crossing one another at right-
angles. Similar grid plans extend back
to Roman times (as at Caerwent or
at Chester), and were again repeated
in Anglo-Saxon *burhs* such as
Wareham (Dorset) and Wallingford
(Berkshire).

New towns were usually created
for economic purposes. A Saxon
abbot of St Albans, for example,
diverted Watling Street to pass
through a new market-place at his
abbey's gate. A town as well as an
abbey was planted on the site of the
battle of Hastings, and in thirteenth-
century Wales a new town was laid
out along the main road between
Cardiff and Neath, at Cowbridge.
Castles, too, particularly when

planted in open country, needed a
local market for supplies of all kinds.

The medieval arrangement of
creating a *bastide* or new town was
comparatively simple. It was a system
designed for the mutual benefit of the
king, the landowner, and the new
townsfolk, and it provided an efficient
way of marketing surplus food and
other goods. The landowner would
charge a rent for a building plot (a
burgage), on which the settler (a
burgess) would erect his house and
shop, which were often combined.
The king would be petitioned to
grant a weekly market and at least
one fair a year, and the burgesses
might sometimes be given royal
permission to collect a tax to build
defences with responsibility to
provide their own local protection.

A burgess was a free man, able to
acquire property and to devote

*Monpazier in south-west France was one of
King Edward I's fortified town plantations in
Gascony. This view shows the market square
of the* bastide *established in 1284
(Photograph by Peter Humphries).*

himself to his craft or to the buying
and selling of goods, without the
burdens of labour services to his lord
which were common in the
countryside. In many cases, the
burgesses would collectively elect
their mayor and council to manage
urban affairs. Elsewhere, as at Flint,
the constable of the castle often
served as the mayor of the town.

Over seventy *bastides* were
planted in south-western France in
the late thirteenth century, particularly
in English-held Gascony. King Edward I
was involved with such plantations,
and he had met with striking success.
In his conquest of north Wales, the
town plantations such as Flint,
Caernarfon, and Conwy were to
provide administrative centres as part
of the royal plan for total control and
lasting English settlement. These towns
quickly transformed the economic life
and pattern of marketing in the areas
of Wales where they were
introduced.

*Caernarfon was another of King Edward I's
classic 'plantation boroughs' in north
Wales. This map, showing the castle and
the grid layout of the town, was prepared
by John Speed in 1610 (By courtesy of the
National Library of Wales).*

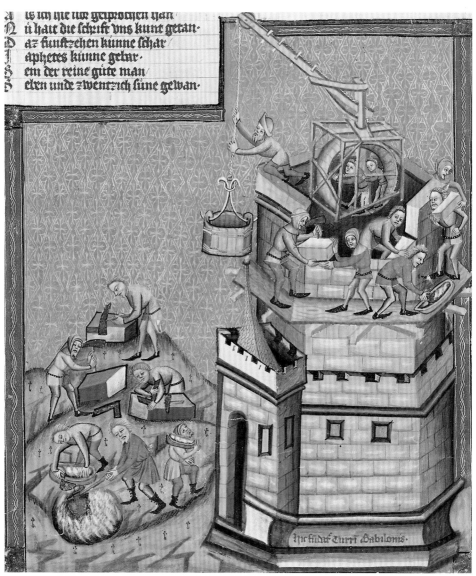

We know from building accounts that a crane was used at Flint to raise floor-joists into 'the tower towards the sea', and that in 1281, some 190 masons were working on stone-cutting and laying. This detail from a late-medieval German manuscript shows men hoisting materials to the upper level of an angular tower under construction. At Flint, of course, all the castle towers were round (By kind permission of the Württembergische Landesbibliothek, Stuttgart, Cod. Bibl. 2'5, f. 9v).

THE BUILDING OF THE CASTLE: 1277-84

In August 1277, 200 masons were on Edward's pay-roll at Flint. Some of these quickly moved on to other royal works, at Ruthin Castle and Vale Royal Abbey, but many stayed to begin building the castle proper. They used material obtained from the ditches cut into the sandstone underlying the site, as well as some 10,000 stones ferried from a quarry near Shotwick across the Dee. The end of the war,

and the sealing of the Treaty of Aberconwy in November 1277, by no means brought the work to halt. Both the castle and town at Flint went on to become a permanent fortified base.

Plumbers were roofing two castle towers with lead in 1278, perhaps the small towers of the outer gate (p. 17), which was certainly completed before 1281. Although some diggers and carpenters remained on the royal pay-roll at Flint in 1278 and 1279, most of the expenditure in these years went on the wages of quarry-workers. They were preparing 36,000 stones at the Nesshead quarry or

Wirral, with twenty masons laying 200 feet m) of wall late in the 1279 building season. ere is no record of payment to masons during 80; but a new limekiln was constructed and the in programme of building at Flint Castle was out to be resumed.

In 1278, King Edward had brought over a master son from Savoy (on the French border with itzerland and Italy), James of St George. Having ried out tours of inspection of other royal works Wales, Master James appears at the head of the sons' pay-roll at Flint in November 1280. His me remained there for seventeen months, at a rate of per day. Indeed, Master James's lasting connection th the work at Flint is also indicated by the grant him of the nearby manor of Mostyn in 1295.

A large amount of stone dressing was carried out Flint during the winter of 1280-81, and the mber of masons at Flint rose sharply to an average 190 during the 1281 season. They were engaged on cutting stones for special requirements, cluding window heads and spiral staircases, and ilding eight arrowslit embrasures. A new vetment was constructed, and a crane was used to se floor-joists into 'the tower towards the sea', ork that was to continue in the next year. Two wers stood incomplete, and their wall-tops were vered with straw as a protection against frost mage during the winter of 1281-82. Very large ocks of lime - for mortar - were paid for in eparation for the 1282 building season. Stones for e Great Tower doorways, well-shaft, and pillars re then being cut, but the walls of this tower still d to be thatched against frost in later years.

On Palm Sunday 1282, Llywelyn ap Gruffudd's oublesome brother, Dafydd, had sparked off a ajor Welsh revolt, attacking the castles of Flint, awarden and Rhuddlan. The town of Flint was rnt, and the building works on the castle must rely have been interrupted. Llywelyn had little otion but to join and to lead the revolt at large. ng Edward was outraged, and intended 'to put an d finally to the matter... of putting down the alice of the Welsh'. He was to assemble a force and gage in building campaigns even more breath-king than those of 1276-77. Llywelyn's death on December 1282, in a skirmish at Irfon Bridge ar Builth, was effectively to bring the war to an d. His ancestral castle at Dolwyddelan in wynedd fell the next month. Dafydd became a gitive, hunted down by a force of up to 7,000 men, d was only finally brought before the king in June 83. He was to face an ugly death at Shrewsbury. e immense castles at Caernarfon, Conwy and arlech - all begun in the spring of that same year -

were to signify the final demise of the native house of Gwynedd.

Following the revolt, and even as building was progressing on the three new strongholds, more work was done on the town ditches at Flint, including repairs after the fire damage of 1282. The masons working on the castle were finally paid off at Martinmas 1284. It was at this time, too, that the new shire county of Flint was established under the Statute of Wales. Finally, metal fittings and carpentry for the castle, including the bridge between the castle and the town, together with a roofing of the Great Tower in lead (replacing earlier thatch), were paid for in 1286.

Although it is difficult to be precise, altogether about £7,000 had been spent on the town and the castle defences of Flint, mainly in the years 1277, 1279, 1281 and 1282. If this may seem like a comparatively small sum, we should remember that the whole cost of Conwy's great stone defences, both of the castle and the town, cost about £14,000 over the four years from 1284 to 1287. This was no more than double the cost of Flint, and - though the castle was largely of stone - the town of Flint was protected only by timber and earthwork defences.

A further revolt in 1294-95 was to test the effectiveness of all of Edward I's Welsh castles. In the autumn of 1294, the constable of Flint Castle, who also served as mayor of the borough, burnt the town to deny shelter and provisions to the Welsh attacking force which was laying siege to the castle, a not unusual tactic of warfare through to more modern times.

Many of the royal bills and accounts for the building of both the castle and town at Flint survive, and we can piece together a very clear picture of the way the work progressed. This illustration is from a collection of building accounts for 1281-82 (Copyright: Public Record Office, E 101/674/23).

FLINT CASTLE IN THE FOURTEENTH CENTURY

Significant new works u undertaken at Flint in th. early 1300s, when the c was in the hands of Edu of Caernarfon - later Edward II (1307-27). T image of the king comes from his tomb effigy at Gloucester Cathedral (B courtesy of the Conway Library, Courtauld Insti of Art).

In 1301, Flint passed to Edward of Caernarfon, earl of Chester, who was later to become King Edward II (1307-27). Over the next two years, works amounting to some £146 were undertaken at the castle. The most significant item in the expenditure was the building of 'a large timber structure, surmounted by a singularly beautiful wooden gallery circling the top of the Great Tower' (... *magnam operacionem ligneam super magnam Turrim... una cum una carola lignea nobili et pulcra*). Its construction seems to have involved the complete reroofing of the tower in lead. Carpenters were engaged to make a new bridge and were hanging 'windows' (probably shutters) in the battlements of the inner ward. Following this work, however, little further building is recorded at Flint apart from regular maintenance. Items which stand out include the repair of the palisade on the outer bailey in 1328, with its parapet completed in 133 and a new hall built 'for hearing pleas before the king's justices' in 1382.

These later items of expenditure remind us tha through the fourteenth century the castle continu to be maintained in good order, serving as an administrative and financial centre for the county Flint. Justice was dispensed from the site, and occasionally it served as a base for the assembly o troops. The county itself was governed as an administrative annex of the palatinate of Chester.

In this fifteenth-century French manuscript illustration, King Richard II (1377-99) is depicted meeting with Henry Bolingbroke Flint Castle. The event took place about 14-16 August 1399, shortly before the king's abdication (By kind permission of the British Library, Harley Ms. 1319, f. 50).

Flint's most famous appearance in history was in 99. King Richard II (1377-99), returning from npaign in Ireland, had been continuously harassed adherents of his rival, Henry Bolingbroke, duke Lancaster. Richard, having moved from castle to tle, eventually arrived at Flint. About the 14-16 gust 1399, 'having heard Mass, he went upon the lls of the castle, which are large and wide on the ide, and beheld the duke of Lancaster as he came ong the seashore with all his host'. Richard scended to 'the base court, where kings grow base' Shakespeare put it), and was thereafter escorted London where he sealed a deed of abdication.

The only other known medieval building work at nt was the construction of a further hall and amber within the castle in 1452.

THE CIVIL WAR AND AFTER

t the outbreak of the Civil War between King Charles I (1625-49) and Parliament in 1642, nt Castle had just been repaired and was rrisoned by local royalists. It was to serve as a eful base for harrying the besiegers of Chester and r helping blockade-runners to get into the city by ater. The castle was surrendered after a siege in 43, but was recovered by royalist troops landed m Ireland. In 1645, it seems to have been retaken r Parliament and then, in turn, once more for the ng. When the royalist stronghold of Chester rrendered early in 1646, the Parliamentary forces nply bypassed the remaining nearby castles held r the king. After a somewhat desultory siege

A drawing of Flint Castle from the north-west by Francis Place, 1699 (By courtesy of the National Library of Wales).

lasting some three months, however, Flint Castle was surrendered on honourable terms in August 1646.

For a time the castle was garrisoned for Parliament with one tower used as a prison. But in 1647 the garrison was removed, and along with other north Wales castles it was 'slighted' as ordered. Exactly what demolition was then undertaken is not clear, but debris of this date was found during archaeological excavations of the ditch near the south-west tower. In 1652 Flint was described as almost buried in its own ruins.

A new gaol for the county was built in the outer ward of the castle in 1784-85, a structure which survived until 1962. In 1919, Flintshire County Council placed the castle in the guardianship of the then Office of Works under the provisions of the Ancient Monuments Acts. The old gaol was later released from its occupancy by the Territorial Army, and the outer ward reunited with the rest of the castle in 1939. The castle is now maintained by Cadw: Welsh Historic Monuments on behalf of the National Assembly for Wales .

THE SOUTH EAST VIEW OF FLINT CASTLE.

THIS Castle was begun by King Hen.II.& finished by K. Edn.I.K. Rich.II .on his Return from Ireland was for some time Entertained here but on his Depar-

int Castle from the south-east, with the Great Tower in the foreground, as illustrated by the brothers Buck in 1742. Notice w the waters of the Dee came up much closer to the walls and towers even at this comparatively late date.

A TOUR OF FLINT CASTLE

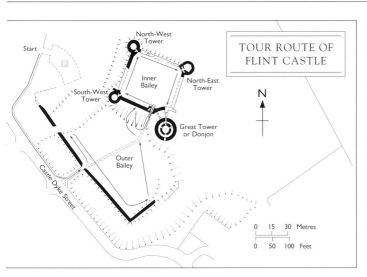

TOUR ROUTE OF FLINT CASTLE

THE OUTER WARD

ou should begin your tour from e car-park beside the south-west wer. With your back to the ast, turn left and left again into astle Dyke Street. Follow the ad, with the castle on your left- nd side. The medieval castle tch extended further out under astle Dyke Street, and originally was filled by salt water at high les. The present grass-covered ope is essentially a modern ature, created when the ditch as cleared out. When first dug 1277, the sides of the ditch ere revetted with turves, ough these were later replaced y local stone.

Now turn left along the ootpath across the grass heading r the slope which leads up ongside a crag of masonry. The ath at this point covers the mains of the thirteenth-century

bridge crossing the outer moat. The builders left a narrow tongue of rock just below water level to carry a wooden bridge on trestles. During archaeological excavations in 1971-74, the timber baseplates of the wooden bridge were found 'fossilized' under the stone piers of a later bridge which in turn was replaced by a stone causeway. The stone

slabs mark the site of the outer gatehouse, of which only a small fragment survives above ground. At first, the gate simply comprised two side walls, but these were replaced by a square tower projecting forward. The tower contained a stone-lined pit into which the inner end of a turning bridge descended when the entrance was closed. The inner part of the gate had a small square tower on each side.

Once at the top of the slope, turn left along the line of the curtain wall. Just a few steps on, looking left towards the town, you will have a view straight up the main street of Flint. It remains much as laid out in 1277, and survives as the main street today, with the spire of the parish church (built in 1846-48 on the site of the demolished medieval edifice) showing above the houses. The outer curtain wall continues, and - beyond the present gap - there is a further freestanding stretch.

The grass-covered gentle slope of the outer castle ditch is an essentially modern feature. It was much wider and deeper during the Middle Ages. The slope and crag of masonry in this view mark the position of the outer gatehouse. Further details of this gate are known from archaeological excavation.

eft: A view from the Great Tower at int, looking towards the north-east wer and the Dee estuary beyond. uring the medieval period, the waters f the Dee came right up to the foot of e castle walls at high tides.

17

A BIRD'S-EYE VIEW OF FLINT CASTLE
FROM THE SOUTH

8 North-West Tower - *There are arrowslit embrasures in the basement, though the upper rooms may have been residential. A large fireplace survives on one floor (p. 23).*

9 North-East Towe *This is the best preserved of the three towers aroun the inner ward proper. It comprise a basement with three floors above, some of which appear to have been residential (p. 24).*

1 Castle Ditch - *First dug in 1277, the medieval ditch extended further out under the modern street. It was originally filled by salt water at high tides (p. 17).*

2 Outer Gatehouse - *The slope and crag of masonry at this point mark the position of an outer gatehouse. Details of a turning bridge, which spanned a section of the ditch, have been recovered by archaeological excavation (p. 17).*

3 Outer Ward - *Much of this area was covered by the county gaol from 1785, until the 1960s. Massive timbers from earlier castle buildings were found during archaeological excavations (p. 20).*

4 Inner Ward Curtain Wall - *This is the best surviving section of the inner ward walls. There were five arrowslits along this stretch (p. 21).*

5 Inner Gatehouse - *The front of this gate was protected by a turning bridge. There were doors at the inner end of the passage, where there are also traces of a portcullis groove (p. 22).*

6 South-West Tower - *This tower had a circular basement, with three circular storeys above (p. 22).*

7 Buildings in the Inner Ward - *These foundations probably belong to more recent phases in the castle's history. The medieval buildings were probably raised in timber, and perhaps stood against the curtain walls (p. 23).*

10 The Great Tower *Designed to a unique plan, there is no know parallel in Britain or the Continent. A basement and parts of one upper floor survive, though there are clear indications that the tower rose higher (pp. 24-27).*

11 Great Tower Chap *This may well have been where Richard I heard mass in August 1399, before meeting Henry Bolingbroke (pp. 14-15, 27).*

A BIRD'S-EYE VIEW OF EWLOE CASTLE

FROM THE WEST

5 Welsh Tower - This strong rectangular tower, of two storeys, has an apse at one end overlooking the main approach to the castle. As the castle's principal stronghold, it probably functioned as a keep (pp. 32-34).

3 Stair - The rear abutment of a stone stair leading up to the wall-walk of the curtain (p. 30).

4 Buildings - This area of the upper ward probably contained one or more buildings. The site of a doorway can still be seen (p. 31).

Bridge Abutment - ...ne footings in the ...f mark the base of ... abutment for a ...oden bridge which ... up into the upper ...rd (p. 30).

Entrance - ...e original ...trance to the ...per ward ...nsisted of a ...in doorway ...ough the ...rtain wall ...30).

1 Lower Curtain Wall - ...uilt in short straight ...retches, with an ...ternal splayed base, ...is length of curtain ...ntains two doorways ...ading from the ...uildings constructed ...gainst its inner face. ...he entrance to the ...wer ward is close to ...e point where this ...all joins the upper ...rtain, behind the large ...ee (pp. 35-36).

10 West Tower - Standing two storeys high, this round tower defended the western end of the spur upon which the castle is built (pp. 35-36).

9 Well - Although now blocked, the well is known to have had a timber lining (p. 35).

8 Lower Ward - What is now an open space would have contained most of the buildings of the castle, such as a hall, kitchen, chapel, stables, and accommodation for retainers (p. 35).

7 Stair - Wooden stairs probably linked the upper and lower wards at this point (p. 31).

6 Upper Curtain Wall - The stone revetment to the upper ward consists of a series of straight stretches of walling extending upwards into a curtain wall (p. 30).

(Illustrations by John Banbury)

The wall as a whole formed a revetment along the inner side of the castle ditch, though the freestanding portion has been much reduced by industrial workings over a long period in that area. Excavation suggests that, at the far end of what remains, the wall curved back sharply to the right, towards the south-west tower of the inner ward (p. 22).

Now retrace your steps along the wall and past the site of the gatehouse. Eventually, the curtain makes a right-angled turn and the eastern stretch follows the edge of the natural sandstone

shelf on which the castle stands. Excavations revealed an original masons' lodge with turf walls inside the curtain here. About twenty-four feet (7m) further out into the area of the ditch, a parallel wall of red sandstone was found at a lower level. Massive timbers lay beyond this, set parallel and even deeper, and may have been part of a wharf.

There was a metalled road leading from the outer to the inner gatehouse. Most of the interior of the outer ward itself was covered by the county gaol from 1785. When this area was

excavated archaeologically, details of the cells were recorded, as well as of massive timbers from earlier castle buildings found underneath

In 1784-85, a new gaol for the county of Flint was built in the outer ward of the castle. The buildings survived until the 1960s.

THE TOWN OF FLINT

At first, the sandstone ledge which was to become the site of Flint Castle was simply a working area where men and materials were landed and assembled. The living area and temporary barracks were laid out from the inland side of the ledge. The camp pattern was arranged as a double square, extending across the line of the Roman road which had led from Chester to the modern St Asaph. The bounds of the camp were marked out by a wide ditch with banks on either side, which were to become the defences of the new town. Until recently, there were eight parallel streets in the town of Flint, running down towards the castle.

A straight line joining the inner and outer gates of the castle itself can be extended along Castle Street and - beyond the railway - continues as Church Street. These two streets formed the main axis of the thirteenth-century town, and there was a market square at the corner of Holywell Street. Two more roads which run parallel to Church Street (Feathers Street and Sydney Street) are also survivors of Edward I's

This drawing of a mid fifteenth-century seal of the borough of Flint was drawn in the seventeenth century by Randle Holme of Chester (By kind permission of the British Library, Harley Ms. 2040, f. 32v).

original grid layout. Other early streets have unfortunately been destroyed by recent development. However, the line of the town's outer embankment is now marked by Earl Street, Coleshill Street, and Duke Street, whereas Chapel Street marks the inner defensive embankment.

A plan of the town produced by John Speed in 1610 shows much of the original layout. It also shows a central market cross, behind which is a substantial two-storey building with a square tower, probably the shire hall. Nearby can be seen the stocks and the maypole. The gallows (looking like football goalposts) appear to the top left of Speed's plan.

The castle and town of Flint as mapped by John Speed in 1610 (By courtesy of the National Library of Wales).

THE INNER WARD: EXTERIOR

aving crossed the outer ward,
ou will find a modern timber
idge leading to the inner part of
e castle. Before entering, walk
ong to the left and examine the
uth face of the castle at this
oint. In dry weather, it is possible
go down the grass slope of the
ner ditch and to look at the wall
ere at close quarters. The ditch
as originally narrower and
vetted in stone to form a moat.

The stone ramp on the right
presents the original approach
the medieval turning bridge.
the wall on the left - directly
nder the modern crossing -
ou will see the slots in which
e counterpoise beams of the
edieval bridge turned; a different
rrangement from the stone-lined
it of the outer gatehouse.

This general view of the castle from the north-east shows its low-lying position on the very edge of the Dee estuary. At high tide, the waters lapped the walls of the inner ward.

*modern timber bridge leads over the
ner ditch towards the position of the
ner ward gatehouse.*

In front of you, notice the
ositions of five arrowslits in the
uch-patched southern wall of
he inner ward. Most of the wall
built of relatively small stones,
ut there are evenly-matched
arge blocks towards the bottom.
he remains of a projecting
orizontal string-course largely
eparates the two types of
asonry. Some of the lower
tones in the wall have masons'
arks carved upon them, with up
o three such marks on certain
locks. Such marks probably

served as the 'signatures' of the cutter and layer of each stone. The third mark - perhaps the light cross - may be that of the clerk of works, certifying payment for the task.

Excavation of the ditch in this area showed that it was initially some twenty feet (6m) wide. The fill contained early fifteenth-century material, including stone shot for great catapults, which lay below the Civil War demolition layers of 1646. The shot could have been abandoned stores, or it may be evidence for military action during the Welsh uprising under Owain Glyndŵr in the early 1400s.

To the left, the string-course does not continue around the

south-west tower, nor does it run along the west curtain on the far side of the tower. In fact, on that side the wall has two courses of red sandstone which contrast with the rest of the masonry and form an ornamental band. More elaborate banding was employed by King Edward's masons at Caernarfon Castle. Archaeological excavations on this western side were complicated by the foundations of industrial buildings (including chemical works) which here came right up to the medieval walls. There was evidence that the river often flooded the area, so that the inner ward of the castle stood on a rocky ledge projecting into the tideway on three sides.

THE INNER WARD: INTERIOR

You should now cross the modern wooden bridge into the inner ward proper. On the right, notice the few remaining stones of the entrance arch of the inner gatehouse. And on your left are the ruins of a porter's lodge from which people seeking entry could be challenged and questioned.

The gatehouse to the inner ward is much ruined, though a number of details can be made out. The arched opening to the left marks the position of an arrowloop and the gatehouse porter's lodge.

There were doors at the inner end of the passage, and you can see traces of the holes for drawbars in the wall on the right. One of these holes is very long, so that the wooden bar could be slid completely out of the way when the doors were open. The other hole is shorter, demonstrating that there were two crossbars working in opposite directions. High up in the opposite wall, there are slight traces of a portcullis groove. The portcullis would have sat just in front of the doors.

Turning left, and walking beside the southern wall, beyond the porter's lodge you will pass four more large embrasures for arrowslits facing out across the outer ward. There were probably timber-framed buildings against the wall here, as well as elsewhere in the inner ward, with some light coming through from the embrasures. Notice that the sentry wall-walk along the top of the curtain continued around the back of the south-west tower in front of you. This meant that defenders moving from point to point did not have to pass through the rooms inside the tower.

Turning to the details of the **south-west tower** itself, on the left of the entrance you will see a drawbar hole so close to the wall-face that its purpose must have

Some of the details which survive with the south-west tower. Notice the circu.. basement with clear evidence for the beams which supported the floor.

been to bar exit from the tower, rather than entry into it. Just within the doorway, there is a lobby with the remains of a spira. stair rising counter-clockwise. Above your head there is the opening of a window over the door. Looking into the circular basement of the tower, the large square holes which once held the floor beams stand out clearly, with eight beams having run in one direction and two others supporting them at right-angles below. The tower had at least three upper storeys, and - unlike the other towers - appears to hav been circular at all levels. The first-floor room had three embrasures, probably for arrowslits rather than windows.

Back within the inner ward and progressing clockwise, look over the low wall on your left. The section of wall which adjoin the outside face of the south-wes tower may have formed part of another dock, since the river is known to have come up to this point. The space between the wa and the tower formed a latrine recess.

Here, and on the other two sides of the inner ward, only the lowest parts of the thirteenth-century curtain walls survive, an

Two of the best-surviving arrowloop embrasures in the southern curtain wall with the south-west tower to the right. Originally, there were probably timber-framed buildings along the wall face here.

e best seen from outside lthough the ground can be ry marshy). The upper parts the walls here were obably destroyed - at least part - after the Civil War of e 1640s, at a time when any medieval strongholds ere 'slighted' sufficiently to event their effective occupation. There is also a cord of a 'large portion' of e south-east side of the stle ruins falling in 1848. he dwarf walls around these des of the ward, as well as ose in the centre of the ourtyard, must belong to ore recent phases in the stle's history.

The medieval buildings, hich probably included a all, chapel, kitchen, smithy, rewhouse, bakehouse, and e like, may well have been ised in timber. They would have tood against the curtain walls, in pattern also identified at huddlan Castle. We might ssume that the kitchen lay near the surviving well.

The line of the west curtain ontinues towards the **north-west ower**. Judging by the spacing on ne surviving south wall, this

The low foundations in the centre of the inner ward are believed to date to post-medieval phases in the castle's history. Beyond these, in this view, is the west curtain and north-west tower. The wall-walk around the curtain was carried around the back of the tower above a thickened projection of the wall.

stretch may have had six embrasures with arrowslits. Two of these survive, with parts of two others. The wall-walk again continued around the back of the north-west tower above a thickening of the curtain.

In the circular basement of the north-west tower you will see three arrowslit embrasures. Two of these are carefully aligned to cover the outside face of the curtain wall on each side of the tower, and the third looks out to the river estuary. Another good arrowslit survives at the next floor level, where the plan of the room (and those above) is multi-sided. There is a large fireplace in one of the walls, and to the right of the destroyed hood there is a projecting stone which was intended to carry a lamp. The upper rooms were linked by another counter-clockwise spiral stair, situated off a lobby contained within the thickened inner wall of the tower.

Returning to the courtyard, you should continue your tour

The arrowloops both in the curtain walls and the towers at Flint were designed for defence with crossbows. In this fourteenth-century manuscript illustration a man is shown loading a crossbow (By kind permission of the British Library, Additional Ms. 42130, f. 56).

along the north curtain wall. Just beyond the north-west tower, you will see that the wall has been thickened on the inner side. On the exterior face, there are projections in the masonry, and this may have been where ships tied up to load or discharge cargo. If you look out, and down to the left at this point, you will see the natural sandstone rock on which the north-west tower stands. Further along the curtain, there is a higher section of original wall extending up against the north-east tower.

view into the circular basement of the orth-west tower. The rooms above were ulti-sided, and there are the remains of large fireplace in one of the walls.

The north-east tower is the best preserved of the three towers around the inner ward proper at Flint. It comprised a basement and three more floors.

The two upper floors in the north-east tower appear to have provided comfortable domestic accommodation, with window openings and fireplaces.

Modern steps lead up to the entrance to the **north-east tower**, which is the best preserved of the three around the inner ward proper. Inside, on the right, there is the shaft of a spiral staircase leading to the upper floors. This staircase also linked to passages which led to latrines. Although the outer walls of these latrines have gone, on the exterior of the tower there are clear traces of where they were corbelled out over the water. The spiral stair also led to a doorway leading out to the east curtain wall, which itself has been all but demolished to the level of the courtyard.

Above a circular basement, which must have been entered by a trap-door in the ground floor, there were three more levels in the north-east tower. Beam holes show the position of the floors, and each of the upper rooms took the form of an irregular hexagon. The ground-floor room had three arrowslit embrasures. Above, the first floor appears to have served as the principal apartment, with the remains of a large hooded fireplace. The second floor also has a similar but smaller fireplace and two window openings.

Passages within the back of the north-east tower, accessed from a spiral staircase, led to latrines corbelled out over the water's edge outside the line of the curtain wall. The position of these latrines is now represented by a large opening within the wall of the tower.

THE GREAT TOWE

The Great Tower stands at the fourth corner of the inner ward, immediately adjacent to the inne gatehouse. You will see from the castle plan (inside back cover) that the curving wall from the gatehouse to the east curtain wa is broken off on the eastern side. We cannot, however, be sure tha the wall continued right around the Great Tower to provide it with a separate moat.

The modern wooden bridge from the inner ward leads out from a stone buttress. This buttress originally supported a small guardroom, and projected out from the curving wall toward the entrance to the Great Tower. The entrance into the tower itsel may only have been defended by a door, with no evidence for a portcullis. As designed, however, part - at least - of the timber bridge across the moat would have been movable, so that it could be drawn up against the door by chains pulled from the upper part of the tower. Timber for an 'engine' to do this was bought in 1303. To the right of the bridge you will see a low wall across the moat. This may have screened the bridge from the oute ward, or it may have been part o the water control of a tidal moat.

Inside the Great Tower, a fligh of stone steps - now partly covered by a modern timber staircase - leads down into the central area. You pass through a pointed arch, which was originally closed by double doors and enter a circular 'chamber' which is open to the sky. Three other large pointed openings are placed around the area, each with three high steps leading to an arrowslit embrasure across a circular passage.

The passage forms a high, wide gallery running all the way

ound the tower within the
ickness of the walls. In fact, a
w feet from its base, the walls of
e tower are a staggering twenty-
ree feet (7m) thick. One of the
rowslit embrasures overlooks
e inner gatehouse and ditch,
1other has a view of the possible
harf (p. 20), and the third
overs the roadstead of the Dee
tuary. Between each two
rowslit embrasures, there is a
arrow vertical shaft in the outer
all. These are the chutes for
trines venting out into the moat,
1d which would have been
eansed by the tide. The gallery is
ightly narrowed at one point by
well. A hole in the gallery roof
10ws that buckets could be
auled up to the floor level above.
nder the entrance passage to the
ower, the gallery steps down,
ith a much lower vault overhead.

Notice that each set of
steps is lit by a narrow
slit through the outer
wall.

If you now return up
the modern wooden
steps and turn right, on
the left you will see
another latrine pit and a
chute rising to a floor
above. Next to this,
there are traces of the
outward-opening
doorway which led to
the spiral staircase rising
to the upper floor. This
stair climbed clockwise,
unlike those in the three
other towers of the inner
ward.

*A stone-vaulted gallery runs
around the base of the Great
Tower. It is narrowed at one
point by a well.*

general view from the surviving wall top of the Great Tower, looking north and down into the circular basement.

The spiral staircase, rising from the entrance lobby to the surviving upper floor of the Great Tower.

Only the first floor of the Great Tower survives, and this has an external wall thickness which is only half that of the basement below. Just above the entrance, the wall is even thinner, with its floor set higher than elsewhere, thereby clearing the roof of the entrance passage. The movable bridge at the entrance would presumably have been worked from this point. The floor level itself is divided into five rooms by cross-walls which radiate like the spokes of a wheel. Each room was entered from the one next to it. There is evidence of at least one threshold of a doorway next to the traces of an inner wall. We cannot be certain if the inner wall was circular like the basement below, or - if as suggested by two cut stones protruding from the generally rough face - it may have been polygonal. From here, we are reminded that the inner face of the cylindrical 'chamber' belo is built of smooth ashlar mason. This ends above the basement a fairly constant level, a little abo the inner arches. Above this, the are several feet of rough stone filling, but there is no positive evidence for any stone vault or roof covering the central space. There must, however, have been some covering or good drainage otherwise the central area woulc have filled up with rainwater an been useless. Three of the radial cross-walls contain latrine chambers within their thickness. Each of these has a narrow horizontal slit on one side of the shaft to provide both light and a draught of air.

THE GREAT TOWER OF FLINT

by Arnold Taylor

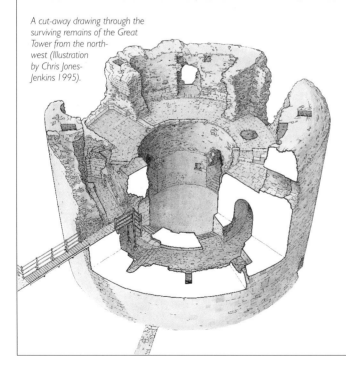

A cut-away drawing through the surviving remains of the Great Tower from the north-west (Illustration by Chris Jones-Jenkins 1995).

The 'Great Tower', the *magna turris* of the records, was designed to a unique plan. We know of no exact parallel, not only amongst British sites but also in any of the other principal castle countries of the Continent. Nowhere, except here at Flint, do we find a suite of continuous wedge-shaped rooms ranged around the outside of what would ordinarily have been the only room at that level of the building. Again, nowhere else do we find a tower of which the cellar or basement communicated, through a series of wide openings, with a capacious vaulted tunnel-like gallery contained within an encircling wall. The gallery and wall had to be of sufficient thickness to carry a ring, or probably originally two rings, of residential rooms above.

The first explicit reference to the Great Tower occurs in a list of payments in May 1281 for the trimming and dressing of over 30,000 blocks of stone, 152 of them stated to be used for building the well in the Great Tower (*ad fontem magne turris*). Building appears to have gone on season by season until 1286, though

If you proceed around the [flo]or in a clockwise direction [fr]om the spiral stair, the first [ro]om you encounter was a [ch]apel. It faces east, had a stone [ba]rrel vault, and has a *piscina* or [sin]k in the right-hand wall. This [w]as almost certainly the chapel in [w]hich King Richard II heard mass [in] August 1399, before he went [up] on to the castle walls and [sa]w Henry Bolingbroke with [hi]s army approaching along [th]e seashore to confront [hi]m (p. 15).

The next three [ro]oms each [ha]ve an arrowslit [e]mbrasure. These embrasures are [off]set from those in the gallery [be]low, so that the wall was not [w]eakened by openings one on top

Above: *Although much ruined, this room on the upper floor of the Great Tower faces east. It has a surviving* piscina *in one wall and had a stone barrel vault. It must have served as a chapel.*

Left: *It was almost certainly in the chapel in the Great Tower that Richard II heard mass before confronting Henry Bolingbroke. This detail from the 'Wilton Diptych' shows the king in prayer (By courtesy of the Trustees, The National Gallery, London).*

of another. It also meant that fields of fire would be overlapped rather than duplicating one another. The room opposite the entrance stair contains the top of the well shaft, and it has been suggested it may have served as a kitchen, though there is no evidence for a fireplace. The last room you enter before reaching the stair again has tilted stones springing from the wall-face at two points. These would have supported transverse arches which were probably part of the ceiling or roof structure.

Evidence of latrine shafts descending in the wall thickness from above provides further evidence for the tower having had at least one more floor.

---

no doubt interrupted by the rising of March 1282 when the Welsh captured and pillaged the unfinished castle. Each winter, the walls were protected by thatching, until finally, in September 1286, we read of lead being cast at a foundry in the woods near Ewloe and guarded night and day until it was needed for the tower's permanent covering.

It is hard to believe that when finished the height of the Great Tower would not have matched that of the north-east tower, and there are certainly structural indications that there was at least one further storey repeating the layout of the surviving first floor.

On 7 February 1301, King Edward I formally granted his son, Edward of Caernarfon, the earldom of Chester and the principality of Wales. The prince was at Flint on 22 April to receive in person the homages and fealties of some 170 of his new Welsh tenants. At Chester, where the prince had spent the preceding days carrying out the same duty, part of the castle had been specially refurbished and decorated

for his accommodation. It looks very much as if corresponding preparations were made to accommodate him at Flint. In particular, a splendid-looking timber structure was added to the top of the Great Tower. An important contemporary account runs:

'To Master Henry de Ryhull, carpenter, appointed to erect a large timber structure on top of the Great Tower of Flint Castle (*assignato ad faciendum unam magnam operacionem ligneam super magnam Turrim castri del Flynt*), incorporating a dignified and handsome ('beautiful') ring of woodwork (*unacum una carola lignea nobili et pulcra*), for the whole of the carpentry and other works, and with any other expenditure incurred thereon; also for making windows and wooden stairs in the said tower: all in accordance with a comprehensive agreement... £28 5s. 0d.'

In addition, Robert of Melbourne, mason, was paid £7 3s. 4d. for adapting the stonework of the tower to match the new woodwork. Benedict de Staundon received £24 19s. 1½d. for fifteen loads of lead for

the roof, and William the Plumber was paid £6 7s. 5d. for doing the leadwork to make the lead roof round the tower.

On or before 25 April, the prince left Flint for Rhuddlan, where he was to receive further homages. Meanwhile, for two days at least, perhaps three or four, the newly beautified Great Tower, with what must have been some form of viewing platform, would surely have been his place of lodging.

As to the identity of the tower's architect, the evidence points strongly to James of St George. From 1278 until 1280, Master James was principally occupied in building Rhuddlan, but from November of the latter year the payment of his wages begins to appear on the Flint account.

What then is the explanation for the tower's unique plan? Clearly it provided accommodation for the highest level of occupant. The prince in 1301 was one such occupant; another, on regular but less ceremonial occasions, might have been the justice of Chester, on circuit to preside at the justice's court.

The Welsh Tower and upper ward curtain at Ewloe seen from the south. The grooves for large timbers intended to support a wooden fighting platform can be clearly seen in the tops of the walls. The apsidal (curved) east end of the tower would have enabled defenders to cover the main approach to the castle

A TOUR OF
EWLOE CASTLE

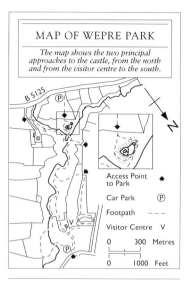

MAP OF WEPRE PARK

The map shows the two principal approaches to the castle, from the north and from the visitor centre to the south.

Access Point to Park ▲

Car Park Ⓟ

Footpath - - -

Visitor Centre V

0   300   Metres

0   1000 Feet

INTRODUCTION

Ewloe Castle is located in dense woodland. In the medieval period this was part of the great forest of Ewloe. It lies about a mile (1.6km) from the shore of the River Dee, and stands near the top of a north-facing slope above two deep ravines where two small brooks, the Wepre and New Inn, meet. The castle is built of a yellowish sandstone which was probably obtained from local outcrops of the Coal Measures.

You will either have approached the castle through Wepre Park, climbing the steep path up from the north (see map), or across the open fields which lie to the south, arriving at a flight of stone steps which lead to the entrance. Before entering the castle proper, however, it is worth walking around the outside to obtain a better appreciation of its siting and defences.

The southern side of the castle is defended by a strong rock-cut ditch with a narrower ditch to the east. Despite both its man-made and natural defences, the siting of the castle, overlooked by the higher ground to the south, is far from ideal. At first glance, this situation appears to have been exacerbated by the deliberate construction of a counter-scarp bank on the outer lip of the southern ditch. Indeed, the crest of this bank is only twenty feet (6m) below the top of the Welsh Tower. But assuming that this bank was surmounted by a strong palisade, it could well have functioned as an outwork providing additional defence. Its vulnerability lay in the possibility of capture and potential use as a siegework.

The castle is divided into two wards. The upper ward contains a strong rectangular tower with an apse at one end, overlooking and guarding the principal approach to the castle. This tower, known as the Welsh Tower, was Ewloe's main strongpoint and probably functioned as a keep. At first-floor level it provided the principal accommodation for its lord. Although some other buildings were built against the upper ward curtain wall, most of the castle's internal structures would have been located in the lower ward. Here there would have been the hall, probably a chapel, accommodation for retainers, the kitchen and a well, storehouses and stabling. What is now an open space would have been crowded with buildings. Overlooking the lower ward, and linked to the inner ward by a high curtain wall, the round west tower completes the defensive arrangements.

29

This view from the upper ward shows the round west tower in the distance. To the right is the Welsh Tower. The purpose of the low wall cutting across the view is unclear.

THE UPPER WARD

A modern timber stair leads through a doorway in the curtain wall into the north-eastern corner of the lower ward. Although the jambs of this doorway have clearly been renewed, this was probably the original entrance to the lower ward. Before ascending the next flight of steps, you should note the way in which the whole of the upper area was revetted in stone. The revetment takes the form of a series of short straight stretches of walling extending upwards into a curtain wall encircling the upper ward.

The wooden stairs cross the upper curtain wall at an arbitrary point where the masonry is now missing. From here, follow the curtain around to your left towards the original entrance into the upper ward. The right-hand side of this entrance has partially collapsed. Looking out across the ditch from this point, you can see the traces of stone footings amid the turf. These formed the base of an abutment for a wooden bridge that would have provided direct access into the upper ward.

Some six feet (2m) beyond the entrance, an internal projection marks the rear abutment of a stair which led up to the wall-walk of the curtain.

With the curtain wall on your left, you pass the rounded, apsidal, end of the so-called Welsh Tower towards the south-eastern corner of the upper ward. This area probably contained one or more buildings. When the castle was first cleared, the slight remains of the shafts for two latrines were detected in the masonry of the outer revetment.

The arms of Llywelyn ap Gruffudd from an illustration of the time of King Edward I (By courtesy of the Society of Antiquaries, Ms. 664).

Little survives of the original entrance into the upper ward, where the right-hand side has partially collapsed. A staircase to the rear gave access to the wall-walk.

In addition, the site of a doorway can still just be seen. It is situated on the inner face of the curtain wall, eight feet (2.5m) to the east of a short stretch of wall which extends inwards from the curtain towards the bottom of the stairs leading up into the Welsh Tower. The original function of this wall, and that of two further short stretches of masonry beyond, remains unclear.

Continue to the south-western corner of the upper ward where the curtain wall stands to its highest level. It is possible that a timber stair may originally have led up onto the wall-walk at this point. From there, the wall-walk of the lower ward curtain may have been accessible, and perhaps another timber stair led down into the lower courtyard.

An artist's impression of Ewloe Castle as it may have appeared when completed by Llywelyn ap Gruffudd, soon after 1257. The view from the south-east shows the Welsh Tower dominating the upper ward. The form of the bridge entrance is of necessity entirely conjectural (Illustration by Chris Jones-Jenkins 1994).

THE WELSH TOWER

The Welsh Tower remains the most prominent feature at Ewloe. Before climbing the stairs to the entrance, however, you should stand back and examine this outer southern face.

There are four square grooves in the top of the masonry (which are easier to see from the opposite side of the ditch). Another groove was found at the top of the west wall of the tower. Originally, the masonry of the tower would have stood to a greater height than it does today, and probably rose to a series of battlements. The four surviving grooves would have been the holes for large timbers supporting a fighting platform or *hourd*, extending out from the wall face just below the original wall-walk. The *hourd* timbers may have been supported by angle braces fixed into the wall at a slightly lower level. The *hourd* is unlikely to have been a permanent feature, but only used in time of need when the castle was vulnerable to attack.

Also in this southern wall face, to the right and at the same level as the top of the doorway, is a narrow window. This provided light to a stairway ascending within the thickness of the wall from the entrance opening to the original wall-walk. Below this narrow opening, the larger rectangular window provided the only light on this side of the tower for the principal apartment on the first floor.

At the bottom of the steps leading up to the tower entrance you can see what appears to be the lowest stone of each of the medieval door jambs. Such a doorway would have led into an

APSIDAL TOWERS AND THE WELSH CASTLE PLAN

Unlike their English contemporaries, thirteenth-century Welsh stone castles tended to be of irregular plan, a pattern frequently dictated by the topography of their naturally rocky sites. Little account was taken of the need to provide flanking fire between towers and along the line of curtain walls. Towers were seen as distinctive strongpoints in their own right with curtain walls doing no more than defining an enclosure. Natural defence was supplemented by strong rock-cut ditches. Entrances tended to take the form of an unsophisticated opening through the curtain, and gatehouses were rare.

Welsh castle towers were, with one exception, of just two storeys, consisting of a basement with the principal apartment above. They could be rectangular, round, or - as with the Welsh Tower at Ewloe - apsidal. The use of elongated apsidal towers is a peculiarly Welsh characteristic. Only one comparable tower exists in an English context but this may provide a clue to the function of the Welsh towers. At Helmsley in Yorkshire the apsidal end

of the keep, dated to around 1200, projects forward from the curtain and provided flanking fire along the line of the adjacent walls.

The curving apsidal ends of the keeps at Ewloe and Carndochan castles, along with the two towers at Castell y Bere, all provided a broad field of fire, from battlement level, over the vulnerable line of approach to the castle. Castell y Bere is known to have been built from 1221 onwards.

The one great Welsh gatehouse at Criccieth, dating to the 1230s, consists of two elongated apsidal towers, standing side by side. At castles, such as Dinas Brân and Caergwrle, this shape is used, in foreshortened form, for mural towers and is more appropriately described as an elongated "D".

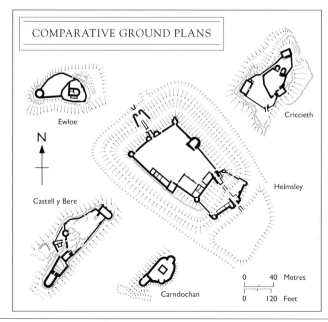

COMPARATIVE GROUND PLANS

Ewloe

N

Castell y Bere

Carndochan

Criccieth

Helmsley

0   40   Metres

0   120 Feet

closed stairway, and the wall on
ur left must have stood to a
uch greater height than it does
day. The stairs, of which the
esent ones are later replacements,
d up to the entrance to the
wer.

*the bottom of the steps leading up to
Welsh Tower, the lowest stones of
at appear to be medieval door jambs
vive.*

On the right of the doorway
opening, you will see a deep slot.
This was probably lined with
timber and would have held a
wooden drawbar to secure the
door. At the inner end of the
doorway passage, there is no
evidence for a further door
leading into the main first-floor
chamber. To your right, the
stairway leads up to the wall-
walk level.

The thirteenth-century wall-
walk would have been higher
than the present viewing
platform, which is set at an
arbitrary level determined by the
height of the surviving masonry.
However, the end of the viewing

platform is at the apex of the
rounded end of the tower. Here
you can appreciate how, from
battlement level, the curvature
would have enabled covering fire
all along the main approach to
the castle. It is in this curvature,
too, that the Welsh Tower differs
from what would otherwise have
been a more normal rectangular
castle keep.

*The stairway rising within the
thickness of the wall up to the
wall-walk on the Welsh Tower.*

*An artist's impression of
the Welsh Tower as it
may have appeared
about 1260. Although
the roof looks set
particularly low into the
walls of the tower, there
is clear evidence for this
in the surviving fabric
(Illustration by Chris
Jones-Jenkins 1994).*

From this high-level viewpoint, you will see that the tower you are now looking into consisted of a basement, with the principal apartment at first-floor level. There is no evidence for any window openings in the basement, although these could have been in the missing north wall. A comparison with other towers of the period suggests that the basement space would indeed have been unlit. It was probably used for storage, and would only have been accessible by a trap door and ladder from the first floor. The function and date of the walls dividing up the basement are not known. It is possible that part of this masonry may be original, and it perhaps supported a hearth in the main chamber above.

A line of holes around the south-eastern end of the tower (visible from the northern side of the tower) marks the position of the timber joists supporting the first floor. The round-headed window you can see at first-floor level in the west wall may, like that in the south wall, have had a rectangular external opening. Both windows have seats on either side of the embrasure.

A general view down into the Welsh Tower from the high-level viewpoint on the wall-walk.

The Welsh Tower from the north, showing the line of holes representing the position of the floor joists around the south-eastern end of the tower.

To the right of the window in the west wall, the left-hand jamb of a doorway survives. The door led into a passage, and may have given access to a wall linking this corner of the tower to the upper ward curtain. Alternatively, the passage may have turned the corner, extending east in the thickness of the now missing north wall. Indeed, when the north wall was first consolidated, there were indications of a possible latrine chute in the thickness of the masonry some twelve feet (3.7m) east of the north-western corner of the tower.

In the upper part of the tower, you can see the line of the original roof, with a triangular gutter through the wall at the eaves level on the south side. The line of the eaves is very clear all along the southern wall of the tower. Note that the roof line on the west wall is steeper on the right (north) than on the left, indicating that the roof would have had an asymmetrical pitch. The outer wall of the tower originally provided protection to the roof rising above it to a higher battlement level.

You should now return to the courtyard level. As you make your way back to the stairs leading down to the lower ward, note that the surviving section of the north wall of the tower, unlike any of its other walls, has a splayed base. This provided additional structural stability on this, its down-slope, side.

THE LOWER WARD

ost of the buildings in the lower
ard would probably have been
mber constructions. They were
rhaps arranged around the
urtyard and raised against the
one curtain wall. Water was
pplied from a well on the
uthern side of the enclosure.
though it is now blocked, the
ell is known to have had a
mber lining.

Judging by the surviving
ction of the south wall, where it
eets the round west tower, the
ter curtain must have stood to
considerable height. Externally,
e wall has a splayed base. Since
ey are bonded together, the
rtain wall and the west tower
ere clearly built as one
peration. However, both ends of
e lower ward curtain abut that
f the upper ward, providing a
ear indication that it was built
a second stage of the
onstruction works. An additional

The abutment of the lower ward curtain in the south-eastern corner where it joins the upper ward.

revetment was added where the
two walls met at the south-eastern
corner of the lower ward.

You should now follow the
northern curtain (to your right),
and walk around from the
entrance to the lower ward
towards the west tower. Like the
upper ward curtain, this stretch of
walling is built in a number of
short straight sections. Just
beyond the end of the first

section, you will come to a
narrow opening through the wall
which may have been a doorway
leading from one of the buildings
constructed against the curtain
wall, perhaps to a latrine. Near
the west tower, you come to
another opening with only its left
jamb surviving. The present gap is
clearly much wider than the
medieval original, though once
again it may have been associated
with a building constructed
against the curtain wall.

THE WEST TOWER

This round tower defended the
western end of the spur upon
which the castle is built. There is
no public access to the interior of
the tower, though much can be
appreciated from external views.
Standing back within the lower
ward, you will see that the lower
part of the tower has been built
against the face of the rock. In the
thirteenth century, access to the

general view of the lower ward with the round west tower in the distance.

tower would have been gained from the wall-walk of the curtain and probably via a timber stair in the south-western corner of the lower ward. This stair would have extended up to a flight of stone steps, which you can just see in the southern wall at first-floor level, and in turn these led to the upper level of the tower.

You should now leave the interior of the castle by the way you came in, and make your way around to the outer face of the round tower. The exterior of the curtain, with its splayed base, is now on your left. Much of the platform you are walking along was built up when rubble and soil were dumped down this slope during the clearance and consolidation of the site. At the time the castle was built, the ground here would have sloped steeply downwards below the foot of the walls.

Having reached the western end of the castle, you should look up at the ragged end of the masonry extending up the full height of the tower. Half way up and about one foot (0.3m) back from the outer face, you can just see the end of a piece of decayed oak which acted as a strengthening or scaffolding timber. If you continue round to the furthest side of the ditch, and then look back into the tower, near the top you can see a groove in the masonry which would have taken the roof.

Close to the bottom of the visible section of wall, there is a rectangular recess, with stone dressings on its left and below it to the right. This appears to be all that remains of a window seat, perhaps part of a window which was initially planned but abandoned during the building of the tower. The basement was probably unlit and only accessible by a trapdoor from the first floor.

Having completed this tour, you can either return to the path leading back down into Wepre Park, or continue back to the entrance leading out into the field to the south. If taking this second route, you should note, on your left, the counter-scarp bank on the southern side of the main castle ditch.

FURTHER READING

Acknowledgement
Both authors would like to pay tribute to the earlier work of Dr Arnold Taylor, particularly his studies (published and unpublished) on Flint. Dr Taylor has provided valuable comments on the entire text of this guide.

R. Avent, *Cestyll Tywysogion Gwynedd - Castles of the Princes of Gwynedd* (Cardiff 1983).

O. E. Craster, 'The Supposed Outer Ditch of Flint Castle', *Flintshire Historical Society Journal*, **22** (1965-66), 71-74.

R. R. Davies, *Conquest, Coexistence, and Change: Wales 1063-1415* (Oxford 1987); reprinted in paperback as, *The Age of Conquest: Wales 1063-1415* (Oxford 1991).

J. G. Edwards, 'The Name of Flint Castle', *English Historical Review*, **29** (1914), 315-17.

J. G. Edwards, 'The Building of Flint', *Flintshire Historical Society Publications*, **12** (1951-52), 5-20.

H. R. Hannaford, 'Flint Castle: Excavations to the West of the Castle, 1988', *Archaeology in Wales*, **33** (1993), 30-33.

W. J. Hemp, 'Ewloe Castle and the Welsh Castle Plan', *Y Cymmrodor*, **39** (1928), 4-12.

W. J. Hemp, *Ewloe Castle* (HMSO, London 1929).

W. J. Hemp, *Flint Castle* (HMSO, London 1929).

D. J. C. King, 'The Donjon of Flint', *Journal of the Chester and North Wales Architectural, Archaeological and Historical Society*, **45** (1958), 61-69.

J. E. Lloyd, 'Edward I. and the County of Flint', *Flintshire Historical Society Publications*, **6** (1916-1917), 15-25.

T. J. Miles, 'Flint: Excavations at the Castle and on the Town Defences 1971-74', *Archaeologia Cambrensis*, **145** (1996), 67-151.

M. Prestwich, *Edward I* (London 1988).

A. J. Taylor, 'The Building of Flint: A Postscript', *Flintshire Historical Society Publications*, **17** (1957), 34-41.

A. J. Taylor, 'Castle-Building in Wales in the Later Thirteenth Century: The Prelude to Construction', in E. M. Jope, editor, *Studies in Building History* (London 1961), 104-33.

A. J. Taylor, 'The Earliest Burgesses of Flint and Rhuddlan', *Flintshire Historical Society Journal*, **27** (1978-79), 152-60.

A. J. Taylor, 'Scorched Earth at Flint in 1294', *Flintshire Historical Society Journal*, **30** (1981-82), 89-105.

A. J. Taylor, *Studies in Castles and Castle-Building* (London 1985).

A. J. Taylor, *The Welsh Castles of Edward I* (London 1986).

T. F. Tout, 'Flintshire: Its History and Its Records', *Flintshire Historical Society Publications*, **1** (1911), 5-38.

N. Tucker, 'The Final Sieges of Flint', *Flintshire Historical Society Journal*, **24** (1969-70), 44-55.